# WHITE PAPER

# WHITE PAPER.

Poems by

## George Starbuck

An Atlantic Monthly Press Book
Little, Brown and Company · Boston · Toronto

LIBRARY OF CONGRESS CATALOG CARD NO. 66-22682

FIRST EDITION

Versions of these poems appeared originally in *Arena*, the *Atlantic*, *Chelsea Review*, *Harper's*, *Identity*, *Micromegas*, the *New Yorker*, *Noble Savage*, *North American Review*, *Poetry*, *Voices*, and *Yale Review*. Magazines have requested particular acknowledgment as follows:

The poems "See America First," "The Starry Night," "The Skindivers," "Pit Viper," "Out in the Cold," "The Unhurried Traveler in Boston" and "Ballade of the Mislaid Worksheet" appeared originally in the *New Yorker*.

The poems "Elegy," "For an American Burial," "From Baudelaire: Spleen et Ideal XXVII," "Of Late," "Poem Issued by Me to Congressmen" and "Pro Forma" appeared originally in *Poetry*.

ATLANTIC–LITTLE, BROWN BOOKS
ARE PUBLISHED BY
LITTLE, BROWN AND COMPANY
IN ASSOCIATION WITH
THE ATLANTIC MONTHLY PRESS

*Published simultaneously in Canada
by Little, Brown & Company (Canada) Limited*

PRINTED IN THE UNITED STATES OF AMERICA

more from than to

*Judy*

# CONTENTS

—◆—

# WHITE PAPER

# BALLADE OF THE GOLDEN RULE

## (To Lord Russell)

WHEN the fat priest looks up from his oolong
and tells me that Mercy shineth in God's sight
in the voice of a three-year-old coached in a popular song,
he tells me right, although he has no right.
And when Carolyi, his fingers in permanent flight
and his words unable to get back where they belong,
tells me the simple truth it cost him sight,
sons, daughters to learn, he tells me wrong.

When the well-heeled escapee from Hong Kong
graces his talk on the Menace of Communist Might
with the thought that Only Our Love Shall Make Us Strong,
he tells me right, although he has no right.
And when Big Henry, back at his broom in spite
of the Ford ignition coil and the jackboot thong,
gives me an unimpassioned black-and-white
of the old As Is as it is, he tells me wrong.

There is no justice. The lump with the HueyLong
galluses and the diffidence of a Birchite,
beating the Book like his own personal gong,
can tell me right, though he has no more right
to gospel at me than to sleep at night
while the night does business elsewhere hammer and tong.
But teach the boy, show him the appetite
of the air for his own screams, he'll tell me wrong.

L'envoi
Bertie, you mathematical blatherskite,
you knew all this. You held fast for so long.
You seemed so uninstructible in the right
of wrongs to exact their modicum of wrong.

3

# OF LATE

"STEPHEN SMITH, University of Iowa sophomore, burned
what he said was his draft card"
and Norman Morrison, Quaker, of Baltimore Maryland,
burned what he said was himself.
You, Robert McNamara, burned what you said was a concen-
tration
of the Enemy Aggressor.
No news medium troubled to put it in quotes.

And Norman Morrison, Quaker, of Baltimore Maryland,
burned what he said was himself.
He said it with simple materials such as would be found in
your kitchen.
In your office you were informed.
Reporters got cracking frantically on the mental disturbance
angle.
So far nothing turns up.

Norman Morrison, Quaker, of Baltimore Maryland, burned,
and while burning, screamed.
No tip-off. No release.
Nothing to quote, to manage to put in quotes.
Pity the unaccustomed hesitance of the newspaper editorialists.
Pity the press photographers, not called.

Norman Morrison, Quaker, of Baltimore Maryland, burned
and was burned and said
all that there is to say in that language.
Twice what is said in yours.
It is a strange sect, Mr. McNamara, under advice to try
the whole of a thought in silence, and to oneself.

## EXPOSTULATION AND REPLY

M<sub>AN</sub> don't bug me with your stockpiles and witch hunts.
O.K. it stinks. So, turn off the radio.
Let em eat worms. But doesn't it gas you though,
Like you're nine and they've told you just this once
You can stay up late for the Conelrad Show?
                                                    No.
Rather as if I was five, and off at camp;
As if no sound on the night air was friendly;
Nothing but emptiness riding the roof tree;
Nothing incarnate nuzzling against the damp
Edge of the tent. Or I wake with the old cramp
Lashing my leg and the old sweat drenching me,
Locked in the arms of the no one I might see
Sleeping there in the light of the bedside lamp.

5

# BUT THAT I HAVE BAD DREAMS

Nᴏᴛ the obscene beefiness of the fenceposts holds him,
but the exquisiteness of the barbed wire.
A late Vogue model casually centerfolds him
over her shoulder and carts him into the fire
ceaselessly accomplishing the purification of Buchenwald.
His sleep mask is upon him, he guzzles flame like a scalding
      brine,
and this and its freight of dead, the tallowed and hair-stuck
      bones, is called
Scheme of the Dream Devoutly to Be Dreamt, Study Nine.

He is my highschool English teacher Mr. Sales,
late chief of a J.A.G. Graves-registration team.
It is 1946.  This night again he fails
and swirls in the old white rapids, the only dream:
dusk at the Pullman window — cloudscape fading — the wires
      astream —
convulvulate once more with nightingales.

## BIRMINGHAM.  PRIVATE BUSINESS

Finally.  The rotation orders cut,
put into action, one set pocketed,
I stood in a Bremerhaven staging shed
and felt like this.  Or not exactly, but
I tell it that way and you take it.  Slut.
Pig.  Schatz.  And sink here with me into the red
leather stickier in the heat than bed,
pending the last licked folded and pasted shut

thing: what he comes out brandishing: the smile
of our guardian guide and Alabama lawyer.
I stood there gawking at her; they swung in freight.
USS *Upshur*, sweaty as a destroyer.
Exalted, crushed, loving again too late,
you will be irresistible a while.

# JUST A LITTLE OLD SONG

But what's that under the catalpa blossom
that just went pop and rolled over with a sigh?

Lift up your crinoline, Cindy, hurry on by;
only a possum could play such stinking possum.

God's in his heaven up in the heavy gossamer.
Nothing but blessings tumble out of the sky.

Nothing but wonders well from the sullen bessemer.
Never you scrunch your shoulders, never you cry.

Bad man stammer and fumble when you address him.
Your little foot go swathed in a gauze of Yes'm.

Wolf back away a safe infinitessim,
lolling the laggard lip, the yellow eye.

# PRO FORMA

THE Law is
   possibly the kindest
     form of death.

The Letter
   killeth, but the Spirit
     deadeneth

to any
   but its own mellifluous
     waste of breath.

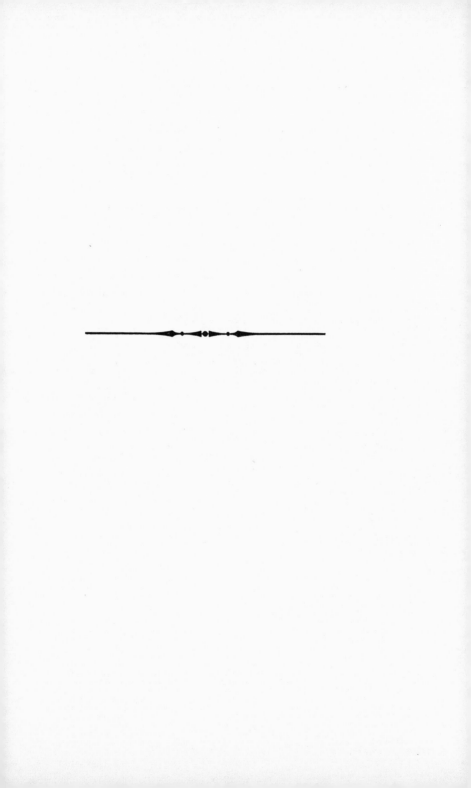

## SCENE OF THE ACCIDENT

THE man is dead.
Turn to another.
That holy father
giving the nod —
he should thank God
he can't tell whether
his kind of bother
has profited.

What runts and sports
we do save breed
business and bread
for our cohorts.

Business and bread.
It takes all sorts.

# THE DEPOSITION

His mouth hangs like a socket from which some noise
appropriate to it has been disconnected.
Evidence of real violence flakes from his working cheek
like dried hot chocolate.
Whatever he's been through these didn't do it.
The desk sergeant leaning forward looks merely sick,
and the kid back from the corner with coffee for the boys
just ill-complected.

There is no malice in the detective lieutenant's frown,
nor ugliness in the way his fellow officer
shoulders deponent's weight by means of deponent's arm:
nothing here to alarm
the hastily summoned License Bureau stenographer
who kneels, straining to follow, taking him down.

## SEE AMERICA FIRST

MEASURE the miles; contrive
itineraries; none
can make the old connection
West. The way west begun
on the first wagon drive
lies deeper than direction:

white dust upon white plain —

snow on the river ice —

immeasurable rain.

But sandblast your complexion;
go shanks' mare; pay their price:
the land you labor over
sleeps in her gown of grain
and men do not discover
the measure of her twice.

## FOR AN AMERICAN BURIAL
### for Doris, for John

SLOWLY out of the dust-bedeviled air,
and off the passing blades of the gang plow,
and suddenly in state, as here and now,
the earth gathers the earth. The earth is fair;
all that the earth demands is the earth's share;
all we embrace and revel in and vow
never to lose, always to hold somehow,
we hold of earth, in temporary care.

Baby the sun goes up and the sun goes down,
the roads turn into rivers under your wheels,
houses go spinning by, the lights of town
scatter and close, a galaxy unreels,
this endlessness, this readiness to drown,
this is the death he stood off, how it feels.

## THE STARRY NIGHT

Faraway hands are folded and folded
or pick at the threads in the lap of blackness
or spool and spool at the tenantless tangle
of blackness, of blackness, of emptiness.

They are the stars; you can see them flash
like the bonewhite fingers of finicky ladies;
and far and away the depth of their cunning
is distance: a tissue of distances.

Their heads are down, they are plummeting downward,
we cling to our millwheel meadows, their heads
are bowed to the task: no comet commotion
of gazes effaces the emptiness.

On the rest-home porches at paranoid random
great-aunt and great-grandmother jaw like fates
till we wish them to heaven. They give us our wishes.
We cling to the earth and each other's flesh —

And ours is the flaw in the nets of blackness,
and theirs is the task by the great sea wall:
the mending, the mending, the never mending
of blackness, of blackness, of emptiness.

# FROM BAUDELAIRE: LE GUIGNON

To lift such weight — to start
Lifting — would take the heart
Of Sisyphus: the art
Is long, and time is short.

Far from any tomb
Where a cortège might come,
My heart, like a muffled drum,
Parades — da da dum, da dum.

Many a buried rare
Jewel is sleeping where
No pick or spade intrudes.

Flowers are yielding their
Sweet secrets to the air
Of these deep solitudes.

# FROM BAUDELAIRE: SPLEEN ET IDEAL, XXVII
(*Avec ses vêtements ondoyantes et nacrés* . . .)

Wɪᴛʜ her clothes undulating into a thousand colors,
Even when she walks you would think she was dancing,
Or think of those tall serpents the holy jugglers
Weave into ecstasies at the ends of their wands.

Like Algeria, like the flat blue over it,
Like the long swell and counter-swell of the sea,
She lets herself happen with an indifference
Free from disdain or malice:  merciless.

Those eyes, the pick of the polished semiprecious;
That strangeness, symbol of anything; that blend
In which only gold, steel, light and diamond enter:
Inviolate angel — sphinx of ages — star —

The very star her hangdog dark companion
Bad-time Charlie the poet names "stérile."

# FROM BAUDELAIRE: LE REBELLE

An angel swoops from his into the fool's
Paradise, snatches up the sinner and
Shakes him, saying, "You're gonna know the rules
Or else. I'm your good Angel, understand?

Get this: you gotta love (no faces, mind you)
The featherbrained, the half-assed, the off-key,
So Jesus when he comes in state will find you
Spread like a carpet of sweet charity.

That's Love, if you want Love: no pat orgasm
letting you off the hook: it's pure, it's hot,
It's God's own fire: you burn for all you got!"

Exemplifying his enthusiasm,
He loves the sinner more the more he flays him —
The more, the more he answers, "I cannot!"

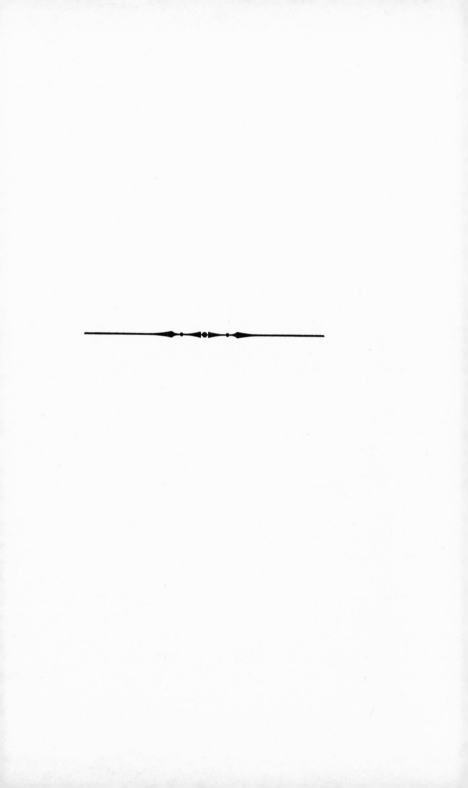

# PIT VIPER

A slow burn
in cold blood
is all snake
muscle does.
The nerves drone
their dull red
test pattern
for days. Days.

The eyes, black
pushbuttons,
are just that.
On each side
a fixed dish
antenna
covers the
infrared.

The ribs, like
a good set
of stiff twin
calipers,
lie easy
and don't take
measure of
what's not there.

The skin's dim
computer-
controlboard
arrangement
of massed lights
betrays no
least motion.
Take no joy.

A strike force
is no more
than its parts
but these parts
work.  Dead-game
defensework
specialists,
they die well.

The point is
they don't choose
livings:  they
don't choose Death.
God save them
they aren't small-
time haters
that joined up.

## MAKING IT

THERE is nothing at all pretty about death.
One does what one can to make a pretty poem.
One writes, in fact, of death — the grace of the poem
does one the greater credit. Why waste breath
in neoaeolian yodelings for love
of the lark's rising? Give us the dead bird.
Or if death gets too easy, take my word,
there is nothing all that pretty about love.

(Not that you less than levitate me, Love,
or that your saltiness has lost its savor:
you are the killings I could carol of
if I were someone more than merely clever
who dared own up to his good luck and leave
the Love-and-Death boys to their heavy labor.)

# TRANSLATIONS FROM THE ENGLISH
### (for Arthur Freeman)

*Pigfoot (with Aces Under) Passes*

The heat's on the hooker.
Drop's on the lam.
Cops got Booker.
Who give a damn?

The Kid's been had
But not me yet.
Dad's in his pad.
No sweat.

## Margaret Are You Drug

COOL it Mag.
Sure it's a drag
With all that green flaked out.
Next thing you know they'll be changing the color of bread.

But look, Chick,
Why panic?
Sevennyeighty years, we'll all be dead.

Roll with it, Kid.
I did.
Give it the old benefit of the doubt.

I mean leaves
Schmeaves.
You sure you aint just feeling sorry for yourself?

*Lamb*

Lᴀᴍʙ, what makes you tick?
You got a wind-up, a Battery-Powered,
A flywheel, a plug-in, or what?
You made out of real Reelfur?
You fall out the window you bust?
You shrink?  Turn into a No-No?
Zip open and have pups?

I bet you better than that.
I bet you put out by some other outfit.
I bet you don't do nothin.
I bet you somethin to eat.

*Daddy Gander's New Found Runes*

RAIN, rain, grow the hay.
Grow the weeds another day.
If I die before I wake,
Skip it.

Little Boy Blue come blow.
    Can't Man; learning a new instrument.
What's with the old one?  Where'd you get the new one?
    Found it in a haystack Man.

Old Mother Hubbard,
Decently covered,
Went to her final reward.

She had to laugh.
Manger was half
Empty and half kennel.

Might've known
Old Church been living on
Principal.

I fired a missile up.
It came down maybe.
Maybe it stayed up.
Things aint much like they used to be.

## LATE LATE

WHERE tomahawks flash in the powwow
and tommyguns deepen the hubbub
and panzers patrol, is the horror
I live without sleep for the love of,

whose A-bombs respond to the tom-tom,
whose halberds react to the ack-ack,
while I, as if slugged with a dumdum,
sit back and sit back and sit back

until the last gunman is drawn on,
last murderous rustler druv loco,
last prisoncamp commandant spat at,
and somehow, and poco a poco,

the bottles are gone from the sixpack,
sensation is gone from the buttocks,
Old Glory dissolves into static,
the box is a box is a box.

# I DREAMT I WENT SHOOTING FISH
## IN MY BARE CHEST

*"When I shoot fish I don't wear an AquaLung — it evens out the odds."*
— IAN FLEMING, quoted in *Life*


I NEVER shoot fish in an AquaLung.
   It might unbalance the odds.
I give the sucker an even break —
The sucker the snapper the grouper the hake
   And suitable cephalopods.
I'm not cast iron: I sometimes quake
   As I stalk with my weapon unslung;
But all advantage I deign to take
Is a love of danger for danger's sake
   And a knack with heaters and rods
      A certain
   Knack with heaters and rods.

I never shoot fish in an AquaLung.
   The man who would is a Red.
If I were Agent and had my wish,
The cad who cheated at shooting fish
   Would get it about the head.
It's not that killing is not my dish
   (Perhaps I would have him hung)
But mechanism is sissyish
Which hedges against the chance the fish
   Will shoot you first instead
      Draw faster and
   Shoot you first instead.

I never shoot fish in an AquaLung
   Whatever the pain or peril.
I never shoot fish in an AquaLung;
   I shoot from the rim of the barrel.
I never shoot fish in an AquaLung,
   Not even the cussedest cods,
Not even the haddock however vicious,
Not even the flounder, and he's delicious,
Not even the shark because Sharks ain't Fishes —
   It might unbalance the odds
      In fact
   It might unbalance the barrel.

# THE LOST TICKET

I TRAVELED with Laocoön
Upon the Lackawanna.
Ten minutes, while his search went on,
I traveled with Laocoön.
His wallet an accordion
File of Americana,
I traveled with Laocoön
Upon the Lackawanna.

## THE UNHURRIED TRAVELER IN BOSTON
(*for Craig Wylie, of all people*)


Out West, how unambiguous:
Avenues march in rigorous
Gridirons like an overplus
Of plusses commandeering us
Into some homogeneous
Equation.
            Here, how out-of-hand:
Alleys John Winthrop's cattle planned
Meander like an ampersand,
Their only gesture of command
A quaint, unmonitory "and."

How hard, in fact, to get well lost in
Omaha, Sacramento, Austin.

How simply effortless in Boston.

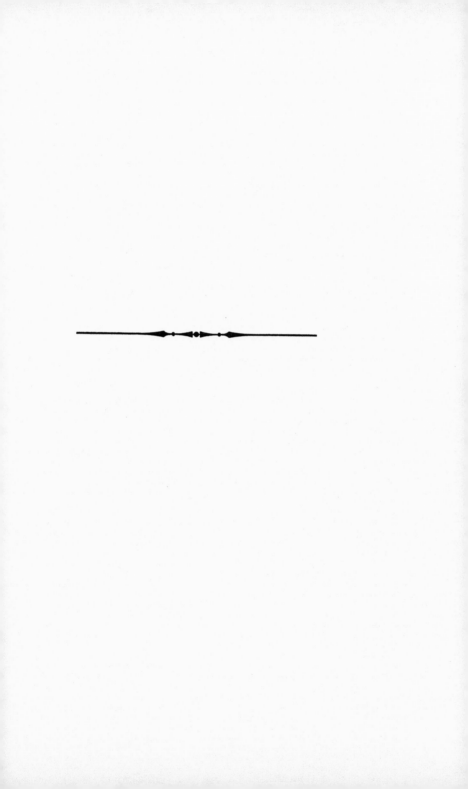

## ROME 1965

Here where the prairies flock to look askance,
where God Keats Trajan and Liz go down as one
irresistible fish-story, priests are in
from fervid Senegal, from godless France,
and here with deliberative circumstance
for three years now the burial of Pope John
in exquisite stages has been going on.
He took a bad name, gave it a second chance.

Peter, thou art an igneous intrusion
across the marble face of so damned much;
thy coziness an architect's illusion;
thy open arms cold caverns to the touch.
Gray plains, you ache for any old profusion
of dogs cats cars nuns Iowans and such.

# SQUALL

Let sea,
then, be deadset
against me; let
that thundering wet
far-to-fathom
gunnel bow and
rail hurdling pan-
daemonium
of pretended
horseflesh become
flesh, become dead
horsepiss becalmed
and sloshing, let
spin from some pet-
cock to rewet
   the sea.

Let winds,
if that's what scratch
in this weedpatch
of rapids, latch
onto what clothes
they can:  scarecrows'
furbelows, chain
shellbursts of nose-
gays, Hurricane
Jackson salvos
of self-sustained
cain until main-
sail, pantsleg, hatch-
cover tarp catch
madness to match
   the winds'.

Let dark
if it will, fall.
Let it be al-
mighty and all
velvet: not some
sly metaphor
of menace or
mercy but plumb
menacing, mer-
ciful: kinder
than what maelstrom
the mind-spider
yet spins in all
his eternal
sweat to forestall
the dark.

# ELEGY

Mosaic. Let there be lashes. The lash obeyed
effortlessly. The mother-warm, ageless,
perfectly fleshed beauty of chaos peeled
back. And the sea take motion. The rest is jade.

Music. An earth. Great verticals disarrayed
in an armed riot of vinestem. A garden still
graygreen-glistening, poised for the spank of breath.
For the rest, Mozart: a grasshopper serenade.

Musk. In an attic darkness among mislaid
columns and roses, the gray and the yellow leaves
smouldering imperceptibly, a green
penny. Out at the curb, a motorcade.

In airless rooms, mistaken fingerings.
How should a draft happen upon these things?

# ELEGY FOR AN INDUSTRIAL DOMESTIC OBJECT

## I.

CRADLING herself asleep, it is a lady
hugging her knees beneath her, heavy-headed
and heavy-hipped; it is a licorice hassock
she couches on, and she a licorice lady

whose maker, as if to footnote his abstraction
of drowsing womanhead, has carved a clockface
into the hassock side, the counterclockwise
eyes of its ten hours widened to abstraction,

the odd pair closed. The silver hand or paring
at half-past-Z-for-zero cannot orbit
on that gapped zodiac, nor the alarmbell
stop stopping, blaring, stopping, blaring, blaring,

nor she herself, for all the sultriness
and heavy hand-to-hand and thick sweet nothing
of the mad waltz she waltzes dreaming, summon
the Prince's nor the enamored sculptor's kiss.

## II.
Hunchback, head in your chest,
all mouth, all circle of gap teeth,
and those stub arms, like fleshy epaulets,
and no hands and no feet,

can it; you are too many freaks:
you are as crass as forty parakeets
whose only trick is to screech, screech.

Black ganglion, absurd
exaction, half-abortion, turd,
last night I dreamt I dreamed
I yanked you aloft and cut your cord
and slapped you until you screamed.

III.
They were afraid I would not like you black.
They were afraid I wanted princesses instead.
Still they connive; they want to take you back
and send me something pastel with pink buttons.
Oh Love, it is not Princesses Instead,
nor Tuesday Welds, nor glittering Barbara Huttons,
on which the soul's deep appetites are fed.
It is the voice that comforts though it crack,
the known dark shape at night beside my bed.

## THE SKINDIVERS

Up and down the beach
gritty as grindstone pound
ball ball ball
heel and splay toe
of the beachball players.

Fitful as hot pigs
bedded into the sand
the red sunbathers drowse.
Ball Ball Ball
hoofs it over them all.

It's ball ball ball
in the beach-pavilion bars,
a polyrhythm riff
for washboard and brushed traps
thundering under the pier

and gone. The minuscule
ball ball ball
of our breaths arises. Still
deeper we settle, cool
and enraptured, a seed pearl

while up and down the beach
and over the waves and on
ball ball ball
throbs the dissolving call
of the beachball players.

## OUT IN THE COLD

All day today the seagulls cried.
All day they cried, if not because of you,
then not at least because I asked them to.
I've got enough poor bastards on my side;
I'm not a Greek, I can be satisfied
to share a chorus with the shrill sea mew
without pretending it's an interview
with souls plucked from the shipwrecked as they died.

I've got enough cold company: the guys
you used to tell me how you used to see
before I came along and you got wise.
Where are they now, in what capacity —
those dear, well-meant, unsatisfactory
approximations of the eventual me?

## BALLADE FOR RATTLE AND BRUSHES

May Day for sure:  new monarchs nod
   above their stricken fetters;
the grassroots fire their fusillade
   of bright attention-getters;
and who's to care or think it odd
if each insurgent gang has trod
under a grizzled awkward-squad
   of aiders and abetters
   as homely as old sweaters?
Who's to complain?  What utter clod?

Busying every floweret
   with touselers and prodders,
flustering flowered flannelette
   with nightmares of hot-rodders,
loaded and looped as it can get,
dizzier than the violet
whose petals arch like a quintet
   of whirling eisteddfodders,
   May is.  The gray vine dodders
and gets more looped, more loaded yet.

Green legions rise through a glissade
    of keepers and begetters —
of husk and chrysalis and pod
    deferring to their betters,
and who's to care or think it odd?
If sod-banked fires of goldenrod
leap to obliterate the sod,
        should they fold up like debtors?
        explain themselves in letters?
Who says as much?  What utter clod?

*L'envoi*

Far be it, my Scheherezade,
from oaten straw or dried peascod
    to be the oversetters
of any ordinance of God
so just, so gay, so iron-shod.
One may be dead as the ballade
but not, as yet, an utter clod.

# BALLADE OF THE MISLAID WORKSHEET
## (for Bernard Weinberg)

WHERE are the notes I made last year
On the flip side of a popcorn package
Toward my perennial sacrilege
Upon the Muse: another near-
Translation of Villon? But where
Is Harlow? Where is Norma Tallmadge?
Norma Jean Baker? Norma Shearer?
What tantalizing curve or cleavage — ?
    Water under the bridge.

Back to my dog-eared Dictionnaire.
Back to my Fowler's *English Usage.*
But where is Mrs. Average
American? Remember her —
Smiling at her discoverer
The census-man — a Personage
At last? And Carole Lombard, where
Is she? And Mrs. Calvin Coolidge?
    Water under the bridge.

Where are the powers I bargain for:
The Archimedean leverage
To raise at least my own dead language
Up? O Edmund Spenser, where
In the wildern woods of verbiage
Hath wonèd wended, and whither yore?
And oomph, and eld, and yesteryear?
And Bernhardt's voice, and Bernhardt's carriage?
    Water under the bridge.

## L'Envoi

A thousand scattered cans of footage
Turning in unison yellower,
A piece of French Literature,
And this, a petty pilferage
On both, are yours awhile, and are
   Water under the bridge.

## BOOK PAGE MAN

Just an imperfect man
Doing the best he can,
Offering yet another cheek,
Not so much meek
As cowed.

Look at him: the poor worm
Doubling as host and germ:
Ubiquitous Iscariot,
Bloody but not
Unbowed.

# THE WELL-TRAINED ENGLISH CRITIC SURVEYS
## THE AMERICAN SCENE

"Poetic theory in America is at present in an extremely curious
state, resembling that of England during the Barons' Wars
rather than that of a healthy democracy or well-run autocracy.
It is not even a decent civil war . . ."
— THOM GUNN in Yale Review

SOMETIMES I feel like a fodderless cannon
On one of those midwestern courthouse lawns
Fiercely contested for by boys of ten and
Topped by a brevet general in bronze.

Hallucination, naturally: no
Era without its war, and this has its,
Roundabout somewhere, some imbroglio,
Even if only run by starts and fits.

Limber me up again, somebody.
In with the charges! To the touch-hole! Wham!
Elevate me, ignite me, let one ruddy
Side or the other taste the thing I am!

This pale palaver, this mish-mash of factions:
How can you find employment in a war
Of private sorties and guerrilla actions?
Maddening! Maddening! It chokes the bore!

Great God why was I tempered of pure sheffield
Unless to belch and fulminate and reek?
Never in England would I be so stifled.
Name me the nearest caitiff: let me speak!

## SONNET ON THE RECOGNITION OF CHINA
### (for Clark Foreman)

Columbus sailed the ocean (misdirected
by a self-styled geographer's conjecture
of the Earth's girth) blue, with a crew selected
from the cons, creeps and crums of Palos Prefecture.

Behind him lay the graying recollection
of Isabel. Oh well. If she could hector
Ferdinand into giving *him* protection,
he guessed the jewel business hadn't wrecked her.

Before him, as it said in his prospectus,
lay nothing new — at most a more direct
way to the old. And though you can't expect us
to swallow that about the egg, he checked

a mutiny, found China (a correctable
error), and almost made himself respectable.

# DEAR FELLOW TEACHER

I must confess I'm tired of these demonstrations.
Surely there must be better demonstrations
against brute force than brute force demonstrations.
Come now and let us reason together like
the Old Man says. What kind of a demonstration
is this from academically trained minds?
Is a stalled freight our cogent demonstration?
Is a blocked highway where some unwashed mob
panics at a mere word like "napalm" our
idea of perspicacious demonstration?
Would Aristotle, master of demonstration,
have dignified with the proud name "demonstration"
this massing of dumb bodies under flags?
Would Euclid have admired such demonstration?

What are we after with these demonstrations?
Accommodation? Compromise? Then let
that spirit permeate our demonstrations.
Was it not Secretary Rusk who said
We have already made our demonstration
of readiness to negotiate unquote?
What could be more amenable than that?
And had we not in fact for five whole days
called off, forsworn, and utterly regrouped
(for that is how we made said demonstration)
our prior and like-minded demonstration
of readiness to negotiate unquote?
Were we discouraged? Did we not resume
what McNamara calls our demonstration

57

that we shall not be bluffed or made to yield
until, in Bundy's words, some demonstration
of comparable etcetera unquote?
Lyndon, I'm sick and tired of demonstrations.
There is a demon in these demonstrations.
I'm fed up with the mere word "demonstration."
Furthermore, I accept your demonstration
that this or that or any demonstration's
about as much use as a plugged piastre.
Like alibis, like sides of beef on spits,
like children in thatch villages of huts,
if you don't watch them they get overdone.
That's the damn thing about these demonstrations.
Let's everybody go out and stop one.

POEM ISSUED BY ME TO CONGRESSMEN ABBITT
ABERNETHY ADAIR ADDABBO ALBERT ANDER-
SON ANDERSON ANDREWS ANDREWS ANDREWS
ANNUNZIO ARENDS ASHBROOK ASHLEY ASH-
MORE ASPINALL AYRES BALDWIN BANDSTRA
BARING BARRETT BATES BATTIN BECKWORTH
BELCHER BELL BENNETT BERRY BETTS BING-
HAM BLATNIK BOGGS BOLAND BOLLING BOLTON
BOW BRAY BROCK BROOKS BROOMFIELD BROWN
BROYHILL BROYHILL BUCHANAN BURKE BURLE-
SON BURTON BURTON BYRNE BYRNES CABELL
CALLAN CALLAWAY CAREY CASEY CEDERBERG
CELLER CHAMBERLAIN CHELF CLANCY CLARK
CLAUSEN CLAWSON CLEVELAND CLEVENGER
COHELAN COLLIER CONTE COOLEY CORBETT
CORMAN CRALEY CRAMER CULVER CURTIN
CURTIS DADDARIO DAGUE DANIELS DAVIS DA-
VIS DAWSON DE LA GARZA DELANEY DENT DEN-
TON DERWINSKI DEVINE DICKINSON DINGELL
DOLE DONOHUE DORN DOW DOWDY DOWNING
DULSKI DUNCAN DUNCAN DWYER DYAL ED-
MONDSON EDWARDS EDWARDS ELLSWORTH
ERLENBORN EVANS EVERETT FALLON FARB-
STEIN FARNSLEY FARNUM FASCELL FEIGHAN
FINDLEY FINO FISHER FLOOD FLYNT FOGARTY
FOLEY FORD FORD FOUNTAIN FRASER FRELING-
HUYSEN FRIEDEL FULTON FULTON FUQUA GAL-
LAGHER GARMATZ GATHINGS GETTYS GIAIMO
GIBBONS GILBERT GILLIGAN GONZALEZ GOOD-
ELL GRABOWSKI GRAY GREEN GREIGG GRIDER

59

GRIFFIN GRIFFITHS GROSS GROVER GUBSER GUR-
NEY HAGAN HAGEN HALEY HALL HALLECK
HALPERN HAMILTON HANLEY HANNA HANSEN
HANSEN HANSEN HARDY HARRIS HARSHA HAR-
VEY HARVEY HATHAWAY HEBERT HECHLER
HELSTOSKI HENDERSON HERLONG HICKS HOLI-
FIELD HOLLAND HORTON HOWARD HULL HUN-
GATE HUOT HUTCHINSON ICHORD JACOBS JAR-
MAN JENNINGS JOELSON JOHNSON JOHNSON
JOHNSON JONAS JONES JONES KARSTEN KARTH
KASTENMEIER KEE KEITH KELLY KING KIRWAN
KLUCZYNSKI KORNEGAY KREBS KUNKEL LAIRD
LANDRUM LANGEN LATTA LEGGETT LENNON
LIPSCOMB LONG LONG LOVE MACDONALD MAC-
GREGOR MACHEN MACKAY MACKIE MADDEN
MAHON MAILLIARD MARSH MARTIN MARTIN
MARTIN MATHIAS MATSUNAGA MATTHEWS
MAY MCCLORY MCCULLOCH MCDADE MCDOW-
ELL MCEWEN MCFALL MCGRATH MCMILLAN
MCVICKER MEEDS MICHEL MILLER MILLS MIN-
ISH MINK MINSHALL MIZE MOELLER MONAGAN
MOORE MOORHEAD MORGAN MORRIS MORSE
MORTON MOSHER MOSS MULTER MURPHY
MURPHY MURRAY NATCHER NEDZI NELSEN NIX
O'BRIEN O'HARA O'HARA O'KONSKI OLSEN OL-
SON O'NEAL O'NEILL OTTINGER PASSMAN PAT-
MAN PATTEN PEPPER PERKINS PHILBIN PICKLE
PIKE POAGE POFF POWELL PRICE PUCINSKI PUR-
CELL QUIE QUILLEN RACE RANDALL REDLIN
REID REID REIFEL REINECKE RESNICK REUSS
RHODES RHODES RIVERS RIVERS ROBERTS ROBI-
SON RODINO ROGERS ROGERS ROGERS RONAN
ROONEY ROONEY ROOSEVELT ROSENTHAL ROS-
TENKOWSKI ROUDEBUSH ROUSH RUMSFELD
ST. GERMAIN ST. ONGE SATTERFIELD SAYLOR
SCHEUER SCHISLER SCHMIDHAUSER SCHNEE-
BELI SCHWEIKER SECREST SELDEN SENNER SHIP-

LEY SHRIVER SICKLES SIKES SISK SKUBITZ SLACK
SMITH SMITH SPRINGER STAFFORD STAGGERS
STALBAUM STANTON STEED STEPHENS STRAT-
TON STUBBLEFIELD SWEENEY TALCOTT TAYLOR
TEAGUE TEAGUE TENZER THOMPSON THOMP-
SON THOMSON TODD TRIMBLE TUNNEY TUTEN
UDALL ULLMAN UTT VAN DEERLIN VANIK VIG-
ORITO VIVIAN WAGGONNER WALKER WALKER
WATKINS WATSON WATTS WELTNER WHALLEY
WHITE WHITE WHITENER WHITTEN WIDNALL
WILLIAMS WILSON WILSON WOLFF WRIGHT
WYATT WYDLER YATES YOUNG YOUNGER AND
ZABLOCKI (Y) IN HONOR OF SMITH OF NEW
YORK (N)

Y OUR poem is issued to you so
you may burn it and so
it may cost you burning and so
it is issued to you. Burn it.

Perhaps no more than a draft
will have as yet been issued.
There have been critical shortages.
Honor the draft and burn it.

Perhaps in your case only
a symbol is issued pending
the draft, pending completion
of the true poem. Burn it.

The issue is not in the poem but in the burning.
The poem is not in the symbol but in the burning issue.
The poem is not in the flesh, even, but in what issues burning
after the flesh and after
action, the sonnet of tension, the absolute sonnet
of quiet guard.

Your hands are full with the plain hardware of it.
Interval. Dress. Alignment. This is it.
What's it to you what some junk sculptor later
makes of its wasted workbreath? This is it.
Uses are what you drill from this hard center.
Meanings are what you burn off into slag.
Cause is the bright and accidental spiral
you plane from it to leave it what it is.
Whatever sudden emptiness may send you
whining like shrapnel through the bars back home,
whatever you drag home to disremember
bloodily and obscenely and at length,
this will be something else. Head down, knees high,
weapon at high port, MOVE. Your hands are full.

Quiet. A calyx closes. Heavy leaves
foreign to you in their simplicity
of outline and arrangement slowly lose
outline and then arrangement. Their red green
and the transparent oranges and blues
of a fragmented distance gone to black,
a darkness is composed. Its black-on-black
reciprocating engine of gun barrels
cranks over once, fires once, and lashes back.
Nothing is here the night so much imperils
as loneliness. Nothing the breathing dark
so much dispels. Your fix upon the known
is on point flashes answering to your own
the way no pulse or persuasion has or shall.

Poem? You want a poem we got poems, Baby.

Bow Bray Brock Brooks
We're the gunners got the gooks.
Pickle Pike Poage Poff
Charlie seen us an took off.

Rhodes Rhodes Rivers Rivers
Give us the job an we delivers.
White White Whitener Whitten
Nobody sets back the hard-bitten
Special Detachment Ran-gers!

Peace, Wanderer. Patience at your hard labor.
Later, almost in silence, and by surprise
must come to you if at all the at night now wept for,
the halfway-around-the-world-awaited rising
as out of a grayed horizon
                              Objective.
                                        This.

Slow outcrop of bone faces. Baring of teeth
In the brief space of a doorway in ashes. This.

Cathay? Santo Domingo? Some such name.

The whole West waits to award you, you need only
(But a figure out of your own squad bumps past you,
rigorous, heavyladen and unimpeachable
upon the work of confiscation. Others
fan into the near distance, smoke-obscured.
Smoke falls
            back on itself around you,
                                    leaves you
somewhere
            a light truck motor labors,
                                    lone
sound of a dark
                March morning in some St.
                                        Paul
the exhaustclouds lifting
                    neighbor and stranger
                                        lifting

as out of its own breath rising)
                                    Objective.
                                                This.
Blackface.
            Implacable.
                        Death his be-all and end-all.
Death his intense
                    meditation.
                                Death his design.
Your poem when issued to you will be Enemy and Response.

It will be crabbed, wrought, strained and in fact
poetical.

It will be your *Ballad of Roger Young*, explaining
how at impossible odds and with what grace.

It will be your *Song of Songs Which Is Solomon's*, saying
other than what it says because what it says
it cannot be saying, just as when

the deathshead in the doorway
who is, Yes, a Conspirator
(he has spilled his guts) and who would,
Yes, have maintained his insidious
cover until the leaves were taken off,
says to you *I*

*am dead. I do*
*not move. Not happy not*
*unhappy I*
*am dead. I do*
*not move. Not feeling not*
*unfeeling I*

And you, because you will *have* your Moment,

you with your flag and book,
you, because there can *be* no such Elsewhere
indolent in the laps of unfurrowed seas,
hammer the words like gold and unfold them *I*
*am soulless relentless remorseless insatiable I*
*shall not be moved.*

Trophies.  In the displaycase of Post Ten
Thousand and Something, Algeciras Georgia,
your own eyes, half-hungover but all there,
in a disturbed reflection over brass
nameplates on walnut:  Trudo, Rountree, Green,
and with the names the years, and with the years
half of a banner head:  VOICES ALARM,
an arm upraised and pumping and cut off
at the white edge of a bowling roster, eight
wide-open-mouthed men straining their neck tendons
in a curled brownstained photograph with whores
(captioned SAIGON, containing someone's brave
tablecloth manifesto GET EM REBS
and one small face worthy of Lippo Lippi)

deserve, sweet Hell deserve, what your sick blood
vibrates as these things vibrate to hear told:
*Didn't* we get em?  Didn't we take arms
an slog halfway around the world to get
them before they got us?  (white shirtbacks rising)
An *won't* we get em?  Let em show up now
callin themselves Americans, oh yes,
sellin us up the creek with their half-measures —
(Dead men around a table:  their dead friends.
Pin-ups of yellowed championship clippings.
Their National Commander with the same
vigilant, just, and just about fed up
glare, as the glare behind you, as the glare
of your awaited turn, your firm stride forward.)

65

Your poem when issued to you, bearing symbols, bearing a
    date,
will be neat, sweet, proper and terminal.  Need it be said this
    late
that these which you read are verses — verses to celebrate
me and my righteous posture, my facts and brains?
Light them, they will at once incinerate.
Burn as you will your poem, the burning remains.

(Here ends the document as issued and read into the record.
But the gentlemen from Arizona, California, Indiana and
Louisiana among others having remarked upon the lack,
strange in a document of this nature, of due acknowledgment
to the Supreme Authority Above Us All; and the gentleman
from Iowa having at hand a suitable Hymn and Recessional;
we here insert in the record the following Expansion of Re-
marks.)

Mine eyes have seen the glory of hard work at least.
I have kept the bore unpitted and the action greased.
Even when it aint a fit night out for man or beast.
What's your story, Mister?

    Brandenburg Louisiana!
    New Vienna Minnesota!
    Venezuela West Virginia!
    Get outa my back yard.

I have seen at least the star shell and the muzzle flash.
I have sabotaged for glory and a little cash.
I have fought my jammed controls right up until the crash.
What's your story, Mister?

    Macedonia Nevada!
    Himalaya Oklahoma!
    Okinawa Indiana!
    Get outa my back yard.

I have walked my twenty-thousand-mile perimeter.
I have cruised at eighty fathoms and a thousand per.
If I didn't they would get my wife and ravish her.
What's your story, Mister?

South Kamchatka North Dakota!
Lebanon South Carolina!
Dutch Guiana Arizona!
Get outa my back yard.

In the beauty of a moment of camaraderie
With a godforsaken bunch of gooks across the sea,
I shall die to make men safe in my society.
What's your story, Mister?

Guatemala California!
Anatolia Nebraska!
Hispaniola Pennsylvania!
Get outa my back yard.

(You take off your insignia. You seek
cover. Maybe they still come sniping at you.
Maybe the outline of a bloused fatigue
uniform is a recognition pattern.

You take off your insignia. Through white
wildernesses of rock to where white water
spins from the snows, still climbing in a white
silence they cut to ribbons with their chatter,

You take off your insignia. The crest
holds you a moment, meeting, of no color
other than that of sunset, their distressed
and automatic redface compulsive stutter.

You take off your insignia. Escape
is a simple melting into the landscape.)

*November-December 1965*

67